COMMON-SENSE LEADERSHIP
A SCANDINAVIAN APPROACH

PART ONE: DEFINING LEADERSHIP

INTRODUCTION

Leading isn't always easy. Change isn't always easy. And I'd like to start this book by thanking you for your purchase and acknowledging the commitment you have just made to becoming an even better leader.

By buying this book, you are already demonstrating what I believe to be two of the most sought-after qualities of leaders today – an openness to new ideas, and equally importantly, a desire to create a better working environment for you and your colleagues. You're also showing a readiness to embrace new ways of working, and that's where I'd like to help.

Over the last decade I've been lucky enough to run my own businesses, manage some great teams, and work directly with the CEOs of highly successful international companies. I've discovered some of the key problems that leaders encounter, and I've developed tried-and-tested ways of solving them.

My goal with this book is to share what I've learned in a way that can be easily applied. I've taken years of experience and made it into a series of tips and techniques that you can start using today. After all, strong leadership is not only a question of good intention, but also of good decision-making, and the sooner you start making positive changes the better.

As you progress through this book, I encourage you to keep an open mind. The goal for most leaders is to create a company that is profitable, efficient, and an amazing place to work. There are lots of ways to achieve this and if you keep moving forward with the determination you have shown today, I am confident you will get there.

Finally, if there are lessons in this book that would be helpful for your colleagues, I wholeheartedly encourage you to share these with them. Remember not all leaders are managers yet. It's very possible that there are people in your team who have great leadership potential and who will be able to support you, as you guide your company towards a better, brighter future. Help them help you, and everyone wins.

WHAT MAKES A GOOD LEADER?

Being a leader doesn't necessarily mean that you're managing a team or running a company. At its most basic level, being a leader means having a vision for improving the way that a business works and having a plan for how to achieve it. As such, leaders can be found in all departments, at all levels of seniority.

This means that there may already be many people around you, who, with a little guidance and encouragement, can help you improve the company's success. All you need to do is to identify people with great potential, and take them on this journey of growth with you, as you move your business and its leaders forward.

But how do you identify potential leaders? What is it that makes a leader good, or even great? The answer to this might seem obvious, but it's a point that's worth reflecting on, and worth coming back to regularly. What is it that makes you feel you're a good leader? And what qualities do you admire in others in similar roles?

My belief is that there are some core skills that all leaders need, and we'll explore these in detail throughout this book. At the top of my list is interpersonal skills. You need to be someone that others want to follow. Someone who can motivate, inspire, and bring people together to achieve a common goal. You also need to know how to encourage a culture of creativity, professionalism, and respect. It's not enough for people to want to work for you, they also have to want to work together.

But it doesn't stop there. A leader needs to be someone who takes ownership of their role, who knows what needs to be done, and who can effectively deal with any challenges they face along the way. They need to be able to learn, to adapt, and to evolve with the business. They need to stay on top of industry trends and best practices, and they need to know when to listen to the ideas and advice of others. And finally, they need to be able to tie everything together and deliver the great results that good leadership demands.

For example, in Scandinavia we embrace what's called "soft values", which means to really care about every employee and their needs. If someone has a rough day, rough month or just feels sad for any reason, you clear your calendar, make time to talk to them, and see what you can do to help them. Taking a soft approach lowers the amount of sick leave colleagues take, shows that you care, and leads to better employee wellbeing.

As you go through this book, I encourage you to reflect on the examples given. How do they fit with your idea of leadership? And how well do you show these skills?

WHAT IS COMMON-SENSE LEADERSHIP?

As you make your way through these chapters, you'll come across a number of ideas that might just seem like good common-sense. And that is partly what this book is about. It's about going back to the basics, remembering what feels good, and improving the way you and your colleagues work together. One good decision at a time.

The goal here is to help you build teams that are happy, healthy, and productive. Naturally, things like offering competitive salaries and health insurance will go a long way when it comes to making your staff feel valued. That goes without saying. But when it comes to ensuring long-term employee satisfaction, leaders need to go far beyond that.

My belief is that great things can be achieved through small, simple changes. But these changes must benefit both your business and your colleagues, and they must be made consistently day-in, day-out. Because, ultimately, your effectiveness as a leader will be determined just as much by the small common-sense decisions you make as it will by the big commercial ones. It will be a reflection of your attitude towards your colleagues and your daily interactions with them, as seen over a longer period of time.

For me, your success as a leader will come down to three key things. Your ability to engage people, your ability to streamline processes, and your ability to prevent future problems by planning ahead. And that's what we'll be looking at in these coming chapters. Common-sense leadership that is good for both the business and your teams. After all, you're only a leader if others are willing to follow.

PART TWO: TAKING THE LEAD

ATTRACTING TALENT

Every leader wants a stellar team working with them. But if you want to attract top talent, you need to be at the top of your game too. That means you need to offer strong leadership, excellent career opportunities, and a good compensation package.

Before you start the hiring process, take a moment to ask yourself what it is that you as an employer can offer. For example, how competitive is the salary? What incentives can you provide? Will you offer health insurance, travel allowances, or a pension scheme? Can you add in any extra perks such as gym membership, free lunches, or a generous annual leave policy?

Now ask yourself, honestly, what it is that you can offer as a leader. Will you be able to help them take on new challenges and gain more experience? Can you offer a good training programme, or pay for them to take professional qualifications? Can you help them fast-track their career progression with new responsibilities and a better job title?

And finally, consider what kind of company culture you offer. Is your office comfortable? Are your other employees friendly and welcoming? And is it a company where people love to work? All these things matter too and having a great vibe in the office can make all the difference.

Once you have figured all this out, the next important part of the hiring process is of course screening candidates. Make sure you have taken the time to create a detailed job description outlining all the key skills your future employee will need. Decide which skills are essential from the start, and which ones you can help your new employee develop along the way. Now rule out anyone who doesn't meet the minimum criteria. This will save time and help you make sure that only the most suitable candidates are shortlisted.

When it comes to interviewing, you also want to make sure you have prepared everything ahead of the meeting. Here are a few top tips to help you make a great first impression:

- Choose a tidy, comfortable room for the interview
- Create a friendly seating arrangement that feels welcoming
- Be ready a few minutes before the meeting is due to start
- Offer some light refreshments when the candidate arrives
- Treat them in a friendly and respectful manner throughout
- Know what you want to ask and be concise
- Be supportive and encouraging during any skills-based assessments
- Give them the opportunity to ask questions about the company and the role
- Outline the career opportunities available and any formal training on offer
- Touch on the benefit package and any extra perks available
- Thank them for their time and let them know when you will provide feedback

These simple gestures will show candidates that you treat people well and that you value their time. It will also show them that you are a thoughtful and considerate manager who communicates well and who listens attentively to employees. This will reassure them that you are a good leader, and someone that they would enjoy working for.

When it comes to choosing which person to hire, you will of course want to assess their skills and past achievements. Reflect on how well the candidates communicated their goals, motivations, and experience. You will also want to assess their interpersonal skills. After all, these are just as essential as technical skills. Think about the personal characteristics they showed, and how at ease you felt in their company. Consider if the person would be a good fit for the team, personally and professionally. And finally, ask yourself - can you help them achieve what they want to achieve?

After all, finding talented employees is only the first step towards good leadership. Leadership is also about knowing how to develop that talent and empowering people to achieve their personal goals. If you can do this, not only will you attract the best colleagues, you will keep them.

DEFINING ROLES

To build a strong team, you need to understand what people are good at, what they enjoy, what motivates them, and what they want to learn more about. You can also coordinate tasks more effectively, knowing you have chosen the right person for the job.

The process for defining a person's role on the team will vary slightly depending on how long they have been at the company. For new employees, it is important that their tasks are in line with the job description presented to them during the interview process. This will help them settle in more quickly and ensure that the role meets their expectations. For more seasoned employees, you will want to pay close attention to how their role has changed over time. If, since starting, they have taken on more responsibilities or expressed a desire to learn new skills, then it is important to try to acknowledge that, by offering them a promotion, a pay rise, or the opportunity to attend training.

Once you have considered everyone's individual roles, you need to also look at how well the team works together. Does everyone have clearly defined responsibilities and are tasks being completed adequately? Is anyone on the team feeling overwhelmed or unsatisfied with their day-to-day work? Are there any skill gaps on the team and would your colleagues benefit from additional training? When it comes to managing people, these are things you need to be assessing on a regular basis if you want to work more efficiently. And be sure to also ask for feedback. It might be that your team sees things differently and has other ideas about how to improve workflows.

The next thing to consider is your own role. How does your management style impact the team? Are you a hands-on manager who likes to be involved in the details of every project? Are you the only decision-maker on the team? Could it be possible that you also need more support? If your answer to any of those questions is yes, it might be time to consider delegating more work and training people to help you with your tasks. This will help them with their own career progression, and it will also give you more flexibility when it comes to reaching targets and completing tasks on time.

Remember, when you know exactly who does what, as a team you can work much more effectively. Having clearly defined roles will help your colleagues take ownership of their work and understand their contribution to the team. It will also give them a sense of achievement, and with the right acknowledgement, a sense of satisfaction.

ENCOURAGING PERSONAL DEVELOPMENT

When was the last time your colleagues had the chance to learn something new? What if you sent them on a course to pick up a new skill or simply learn about something that they are interested in? Investing in your team's education and training can be a game changer. It boosts their performance, gives them a small break from their daily routine, and shows them that you care as a manager.

If you can, try to let them have a bit of freedom to choose what training they get. If they want to go on a leadership course, see if you can make it happen. If they need to attend a specific seminar to meet the requirements of their job, try to find a way to make it more fun for them, and so on. Make education and training a way to inspire, develop and motivate your team.

Everyone has something that they would love to learn, either personally or professionally. Perhaps you could send them to two events – one that you choose and one that they choose. And make sure you don't ask them to cover any of the costs. Give them some cash in advance and simply ask for receipts. That way they don't have to worry about spending their own money and needing to claim it back later as expenses. Remember, always give without expecting anything in return.

In Scandinavia, it's common for companies to pay their employees for the time spent on training.. For example you can usually go to seminars or take courses during working hours. This leads to increased competence and increased job satisfaction. Your employee doesn't need to spend their spare time working on their career, and can instead spend their free time relaxing. It's important to not push people to do work related things in their spare time. And education, seminars etc are work related, as you want colleagues that grow. Not stagnating.

SETTING TARGETS

The goal here is to set targets that are high enough to encourage growth, but not so high as to become unachievable. Your job, as a leader, is to find this balance.

The first thing you want to consider is the type of target you are setting. Is it a financial target to support the company's profitability, or a softer goal such as improved customer experience? Next you want to consider if the target is appropriate. Ask yourself is it something that your colleague can directly influence, and do they have all the resources they need to meet this target?

For example, a financial target might not be suitable for graphic designers. Instead, you could measure their output, their ability to meet deadlines, and how well people respond to their work. But before you set that target, you also need to look at other factors such as the volume of work being requested, the tools your designers have, and the quality of the work they will be able to produce under pressure. After all, it's important to set targets that are realistic in their current work environment.

The next thing to consider is how you will measure your team's progress. First, ask them how they feel about their targets and listen carefully to any feedback you get. You hired this person because they know the job well, maybe even better than you when it comes to specific tasks. And they also do the job day-in day-out, which means they know the exact amount of time and resources needed to do it well. If they say the target is too high, it just might well be. So, you should take their opinion and concerns into account.

Once you have confirmed the target, you need to decide how regularly you want to check your team's progress. Depending on the type of work you do, this could mean a monthly, weekly, or daily catch up. Be sure not to leave it too long though, because you want to make sure your team stays on track. The final thing you want to consider is how you manage your team's performance. More on that next.

REWARDING PERFORMANCE

Rewarding performance doesn't need to be expensive or time-consuming. The best place to start is often with a simple thank you. You'd be surprised how many managers, often unintentionally, forget to acknowledge their team's hard work. Congratulating your colleagues on a job well done only takes a few moments and will leave them feeling positive about what they've achieved.

If a colleague has been consistently doing well and hitting their targets, it might be appropriate to consider a slightly bigger reward such as a bonus, a pay rise, or a promotion. If these types of financial rewards aren't possible due to budget restraints, you could explore alternatives such as extra annual leave or a small gift. The important thing is to show appreciation.

If a colleague isn't performing at their best, you still need to acknowledge their hard work. In all likelihood, they are trying their best and are feeling frustrated about their lack of progress. The best way to ensure that all your colleagues feel valued is to organise team rewards, such as day trips or company nights out. These can really boost morale and will show your team that you know how much effort they are making. If this is a bit above budget, a few drinks at the office would probably also be really appreciated by your team.
Or cake. Cake is always good.

Remember, when it comes to performance, the goal is to keep the entire team motivated. It's better long-term to have 10 people making 60% effort than 1 person making 200%. The 10 people will become better at their job if they're motivated, appreciated, and fairly compensated. Invest in all your colleagues.

PART THREE: ENGAGING WITH PEOPLE

COMMUNICATING WITH OTHERS

Strong communication is the cornerstone of any successful business. It enables you and your colleagues to better understand your responsibilities, your contribution, and your value to the company. In this chapter we will look at how you can better communicate with those around you and ensure that you work well together as a team.

Let's start with the most common scenario: the meeting room. Whether it's a catchup with colleagues or a meeting with management, here are a few things you can do to help everyone feel more comfortable:

- Try to arrive a few minutes early. It will show others that you respect and value their time.
- Try to avoid having a 'power seat'. It will help create a feeling of equality between colleagues.
- Ask everyone to turn their phones off before the meeting starts.
- Keep meetings short and to the point. Schedule another meeting for off-topic projects.
- Make sure you speak in a clear and friendly tone.
- Make sure everyone gets a chance to contribute ideas, voice their opinions, or ask questions.
- Listen to their feedback and make a note of things to follow up on.
- Summarise any key decisions made and agree on any subsequent tasks.
- Take the opportunity to prioritise tasks, outline responsibilities, and set deadlines.
- Ask how you can be of assistance

With this simple, easy-to-follow approach to meetings, you will soon find that your team knows exactly what is expected of them and how they can achieve it.

Now let's move on to the next most likely scenario: the kitchen.
Here is your chance to get to know your colleagues. Make jokes, tell stories, and laugh with them. It is okay to show them you're human too and sharing your experiences will make you more approachable. Be sure to also ask how your colleagues are doing outside of work and show a genuine interest in their overall wellbeing. It will help them feel happier and more

supported at work. After all, communication is a two-way street, and your job is also to listen.

SPEAKING THE SAME LANGUAGE

When you work in a multi-language environment, remember what your 'office language' is. If the language is English, then always stick to English.

When you speak to one of your colleagues in your company's office language instead of a language that only the two of you know, it means that everyone can feel more included. If you choose to only speak your native language, you risk making colleagues feel unwanted or isolated at work. You might not realise it, but you are also potentially making their job harder, as people who do not speak that language are most likely missing out on important information about projects or tasks.

Keep in mind though that people may have varying levels of understanding when it comes to the official office language. Try to be concise, use easy-to-understand words, and to explain yourself clearly. And try to do this regardless of whether people say they understand or not. Most people will say they understand and then try to figure it out later. If you explain everything in detail, it will help make things clear from the start and help them feel less embarrassed about needing to ask for further explanations.

CHOOSING YOUR WORDS CAREFULLY

Always use positive language, as in 'do', and never 'do not'. This helps people to feel supported and it will encourage them to take a different approach to tasks. For example, you can say "if you do it this way, this is the result, which is better than". Or "next time this happens, please solve it by".

Saying 'don't' tends to get a more negative response and can leave people feeling discouraged. Try out this positive approach and see what happens when you speak to your colleagues. Keep in mind that a 'please', a 'would you', or a 'thank you' will have a positive impact on your day-to-day interactions. It will also show your colleagues that you are kind and respectful.

An additional thing to think about here, is to not use apologetic language. For example, if you happen to be late for any reason, instead of saying "Sorry I'm late", try saying "Thank you for waiting" or "Thank you for your patience". It creates a completely different atmosphere.

SHOWING APPRECIATION

Good leadership comes from the understanding that everyone in the workplace is equal and adds value to the company. Everyone is hired on the basis that the business needs someone with their skills, and on the understanding that this person is the best person for the job.

It is the responsibility of every leader to remember this and to treat people in a way that lets people know their contributions are needed and valued. This means moving away from the old-fashioned notion of treating people as 'staff' and 'employees' and embracing the idea that everyone in the company is simply a 'colleague' and has an equally important part to play in the business. How does this work in practice? It means creating a work environment that encourages people to appreciate and respect each other. It means ensuring that:

- Everyone understands the role and responsibilities of each person in the company
- Everyone understands the time and resources needed for a person to do their work well
- Everyone understands how their work affects the work of others
- Everyone treats each other with respect, professionalism, and kindness
- Everyone understands how their work contributes to the success of the company
- Everyone benefits from their hard work and feels like they are a valued member of the team

Companies are built from the bottom up. If you are running your own company, I'm sure you have already seen that a company's success depends on the hard work, motivation, and skills of everyone there. When your colleagues want to do their best, you will feel it, and so will your customers. If you can master the art of ensuring everyone in your company feels valued, respected, supported and fairly compensated, then you will see how quickly feelings of trust and appreciation grow amongst your colleagues.

Though I say that companies are built from the bottom up – it is important to keep in mind that many employment problems within a company tend to come from the top. Do your best to keep leading by example. Kindness spreads kindness. The same is true when it comes to trust and respect. What can you do today to improve the relationship you have with your colleagues? What steps can you take to help people feel motivated and work together better over the long-term?

Remember, always excel in how you treat your colleagues. You need them. Your customers need them. And they need you too. By taking care of them, everyone wins.

TREATING OTHERS WITH RESPECT

In the last chapter we looked at how respect is essential when it comes to making your colleagues feel valued. But let's take a moment to really focus on this and the important role that respect plays in a company's culture and in its success.

Everyone deserves respect. And everyone deserves the same amount of respect. I want you to take a moment to consider your colleagues and the way they work together.

How do your colleagues talk to each other? The most important thing is that there is a high level of respect and professionalism when it comes to people's feelings at work. Is everyone greeted and included in conversations? Is it an environment where people talk calmly and listen to each other's concerns? Or have people been known to ignore or belittle each other?

Unfortunately, a lack of respect in the workplace is more common than you think. It might be the case that incidents are reported to HR, it might not. It is important to get a feel for how people in your company interact with each other, to lead by example, and to put processes in place that protect others from feeling isolated or unsupported at work.

As a leader, you know that you also need to respect other people's achievements and help them progress in their professional lives. It is important to ask yourself if you have created an environment where good work is truly acknowledged. Are you respectful of people's efforts? Do you take the time to hear their feedback and ideas? Do you find a way to thank people for going above and beyond?

Remember, everyone wants to see good results. Your colleagues know their area of business very well. They may have ideas that can boost productivity, and if you treat them with the respect they deserve, then they will be keen to share these ideas with you and to work with you to deliver even better results. If you fail to respect their commitment and efforts, you will soon find that your colleagues have lower levels of motivation and are less inclined to do their best.

This is where management comes in. What kind of example are your top-level managers setting? And are they creating the kind of environment where people are treated well?

PART FOUR: STREAMLINING PROCESSES

LEADING BY EXAMPLE

Be early. Be kind. And be fair. This is great advice for both existing and aspiring leaders. You must practice what you preach. If you want to bring out the best in your colleagues, and if you want a team that is efficient and productive, start by setting a great example and take it from there.

Try to be the first one to arrive at work. Punctuality sends an important message to your colleagues. It says 'I value my time, I value your time, and I am grateful for the role I have in this company'. If you are consistent in doing this, it will let your colleagues know that they should arrive on time, and they will follow suit.

Try to also encourage people to take ownership for their time management. Most people will have a reason for being late and it's up to you to decide whether the reason is okay or not. In all cases, it's important to make sure they understand that there is a difference between a genuine emergency and poor planning, and that the company won't necessarily accept the latter. However, remember that as long as the job gets done, it doesn't matter if they start at 08:00 or 09:15.

Another way to lead by example is to take the time to get to know your colleagues and to be a positive presence in their working life. During my time as the CTO of a financial services company, whenever I went to another department, I made a habit of greeting people personally and taking a few minutes to talk to them. It helped me to get feedback on the work my team was doing and to build strong relationships between departments. I would strongly encourage you to do the same.

TRACKING PROGRESS

Every member of your team should have goals, both performance-based goals and development-based goals. In an earlier chapter, we looked at how good leaders set targets. In this chapter, we'll talk about how good leaders can nurture talent and encourage progress.

If someone is progressing - let them do it at their own pace. Don't push them. People who are already making progress will continue to improve with time, given the correct support. If you try to push them too much, you'll end up with less progress and unhappy colleagues. It's a delicate balance.

If you're working with someone who is currently not achieving their performance targets, try to show patience and understanding. Some team leaders in this position may choose to let the person go. Anyone who knows me, knows that I'm very much against firing people, as there's usually a good place for them in the company. You just need to find it. .

If a person is bringing in enough business to make a profit (no matter how small) after their salary and overheads are covered, then give them more time. He or she is not a cost to the company. What they need is support and training. It might even be that their approach to clients is better long-term and will enable them to develop stronger business relationships over time.

Try to consider other reasons why your colleague may be underperforming. At some point everyone has a tough week, a tough month, or even a tough quarter for other reasons. It might be that they need extra support to help them get through challenging personal circumstances. Another possibility is that the target you have set is no longer realistic and needs adjusting. If several members of your team are struggling, it may be a sign that your business is being affected by external factors such as increased competition, industry changes, or an economic downturn. Try to keep this in mind.

Firing colleagues for poor performance can damage the company's reputation. It can also affect employee morale. It creates mistrust, and simply put, creates a bad work environment. People will think: 'so they will just fire people, with no support?'. If you give underperforming colleagues the chance to improve, or to perhaps try another role, you will demonstrate a certain strength of character that the rest of the team will respect. They will know that they are supported and cared for, and they may even respond by helping a struggling colleague to grow into the role. This is why team goals are also important. All for one, one for all.

Remember, if there's progress, it can always be improved on. Don't give up on someone too soon.

DELEGATING TASKS

Try letting your colleagues help you with your tasks. It will show them that you trust them with more difficult jobs and that you want to give them the opportunity to learn something new. If you start with one colleague, and then next time ask another, eventually your team will start to get a better understanding of everyone's work and how it all fits together. This in turn will help them work better as a team.

The goal here is inclusion. Ask for help with something small, even if you don't really need it. And make sure everyone gets a chance to help.

When you need to delegate tasks, it is often easier to let someone volunteer for the job and get started. However, from time to time it might be better to pick someone to complete the task and then support them as much as possible. This will show those who might not necessarily volunteer for a job that they are capable of rising to the challenge and developing new skills. Be sure to give them enough support. When they see they can do the task, they will get a strong sense of achievement and hopefully be encouraged to ask for more responsibility in the future.

Delegating tasks also signals to other employees that it is okay to ask for help. By taking the first step and showing it's okay to share their workload, others will feel more comfortable doing the same. It will also create a better support system within the team. That way, if you're unavailable or if someone is too shy to ask you for help, you know that the rest of your team can also support them.

STRIVING FOR BETTER PERFORMANCE

Sometimes average performance is okay. But that is rarely the case when it comes to work. Average will not help you attract new business, nor will it keep your existing customers happy. What you should be aiming for is outstanding performance. This is the key to helping your business grow.

Obviously, outstanding work isn't always possible. But if you strive for better results, you'll soon see an improvement. Encourage other people to come up with ways of improving the quality of your products and service as well. That way the entire team will develop a positive mindset and will have the opportunity to contribute to the company's productivity.

By setting high standards for yourself and your team, you protect the company's long-term interests. If you don't have time to do a task properly now, what makes you think you will have the time to do it again better in the future? Don't settle for quick fixes. Make high quality work a priority.

The same goes for efficiency. If you don't have time to improve your processes, you'll soon find that working inefficiently is even more costly. How much time do you have to waste before you realise that productivity is the key?

If you are struggling to get your team to work to the best of their abilities, find a way to incentivise them. Encourage your colleagues to work more effectively and to hold themselves to higher standards. It can be anything from a small treat to a monthly bonus, just to be sure to reward those who go out of their way to make a product or a customer's experience better. Success of the few is success of the many.

ENCOURAGING A GOOD WORK-LIFE BALANCE

In Sweden for example, it's less common for people to do overtime. This is because most managers understand the relationship between overwork and sickness. If people have a good work-life balance, they'll perform better at work. They'll also take fewer sick days. This is because they have more time to recuperate and to do the things that matter to them.

PART FIVE: PREVENTING FUTURE PROBLEMS

AVOIDING NEGATIVITY

Ever worked with a negative or pushy colleague? How did you feel in this situation? As we all know, negativity only spreads negativity, and if a manager has a bad attitude towards work it can affect the entire team. Colleagues might start to feel discouraged, and eventually quit their jobs. They will move on to nicer work environments and try to find a team with a more positive leader.

If you or someone on the team is starting to show a negative attitude, try to address it straightaway. Deal with negativity and problems in the workplace as they happen. If a colleague is in a low mood, figure out why, and try to help them as much as possible. If the problem is that they feel overwhelmed or unsupported at work, look for practical solutions. If they don't feel comfortable talking to you, give them the opportunity to speak with HR and help them resolve the matter.

Remember, if someone seems upset it might be that they are having problems outside of work. Perhaps they are going through a personal loss, divorce, or a health problem. Again, if they don't want to talk to you about it, give them the opportunity to speak with HR or with an external support provider. Give them the option to work from home if they want it. Give them some time off to try to address their problems if needed, and don't ask them to make up the hours. Supporting your colleague is the right thing to do. When it's all over and they've processed what happened, they'll be grateful for your support, and you'll have made another person in the company feel happier at work.

Keep in mind that this also applies to you. If you are stressed, overwhelmed, or struggling with some personal problems, make sure you get some support.

HANDLING CRITICISM

When it comes to criticising the work of others, tread carefully. Discuss the issue in private, tell them what needs to be improved, offer support, and decide together what changes need to be made. When discussing someone's performance, it can help to offer positive feedback at the same time and to let your colleague know that they are a valued member of the team. Remind them that they have great potential and that the main purpose of the conversation is to help them excel in their role. That way, they will leave the conversation feeling positive about themselves and their ability to do well.

If you're a manager, you also need to learn how to respond to criticism. No one likes negative feedback, but constructive criticism can help you improve your leadership skills and management style. Listen to criticism from your colleagues. Take a step back, consider their point of view, and try to learn from it. Perhaps even ask someone else on the team, or a senior manager, if they agree with what is being said and what you could potentially be doing better. It's possible that more than one person feels this way, and you need to take their feedback seriously.

DEALING WITH BULLYING

As a manager, you have a responsibility to ensure that your colleagues are treated fairly and with respect. If someone starts to tease, bully, or harass other people in the office you need to address the issue quickly.

Have a heart-to-heart discussion and find out what is causing them to behave that way. Talk about how you can solve the issue together because bullying will cause turmoil and make other people in the company want to leave. Creating humility helps, as does finding ways to encourage a change in attitude. Perhaps send them on a 'Help Others, Don't Tease' seminar.

If talking things out doesn't work, you might need to take more serious action. Firing someone is rarely the right solution, but moving them to a different department, demoting them, putting them in a different position, or simply giving them other tasks usually solves the problem.

Remember, it might not be immediately obvious that someone on your team is being bullied. And not everyone on your team will have the courage to speak up. It is unlikely that someone will bully a colleague in front of you, so make sure to keep out for signs that something might be wrong.

If you notice that someone is making insensitive jokes, snide remarks, pressuring others, or being argumentative, be sure to step in. Try to keep in mind that people will sometimes try more subtle forms of bullying such as excluding colleagues from conversations, projects, events, and career opportunities. If you notice that one colleague is being left out, you need to fix this too.

MANAGING POOR PERFORMANCE

Let people be wrong. Let people make mistakes. No one learns from being right all the time. It's all experience. When people are failing, help them stay motivated. Whatever they failed at, support them, and help them do better next time. Show patience, don't discourage them, and don't say anything you might later regret.

Let them know that you value their contribution. Ask them what support they need and where they feel extra training might help. Have a kind, honest conversation about what needs improving and put a plan in place to help them meet their next target. By doing this, you give them the room and resources to grow. This is how you create a successful working environment.

By helping your team to overcome failures, you will also become a better leader. While individual failures should be managed privately, the situation can still create opportunities for everyone to learn. If you can understand the challenges that one employee is facing, you can help others avoid making the same mistakes. That way, you will see more long-term progress.

And the same goes for you by the way. When you are wrong, admit it. This leads to loyalty and trust. If a manager or leader can own up to their own mistakes, it helps others do the same. You want your team to feel comfortable coming to you with problems. And you want them to feel able to talk openly about the challenges they are facing, knowing that you will help them find a solution. Make failing okay and make it something everyone can learn from. The more we fail, the more we learn. Fail forward.

ACCEPTING RESIGNATIONS

When someone resigns, first of all, make sure you congratulate them on their continued journey and that you wish them all the best. Secondly, make sure to ask them for an exit interview. During the interview, be sure to thank them for their hard work and all the good things they did for the company. Make sure they know that they were a valued member of the team. Who knows, maybe they'll want to come back later. Appreciate the people you worked with. Whether they contributed ideas, brought new skills to the team, or simply helped you meet targets, in one way or another, this person has added value to your work.

Working with them has made you a better and more experienced leader. Be sure to acknowledge this. And always be supportive of their career choice and personal development. They deserve it.

PART SIX: TAKE-AWAYS

TAKING THE LEAD

- Be someone who takes ownership of their role and who knows what needs to be done.
- Be someone who can bring people together to achieve a common goal.
- Be someone who can learn, adapt and evolve with the business.
- Build a team that can meet your company's needs, spotting and filling skill gaps as needed.
- Offer strong leadership, excellent career opportunities, and a good compensation package.
- Define your team's roles based on their strengths, motivations, and career aspirations.
- Consider how your own management style impacts your team's work.
- Invest in your team's personal and professional skill development.
- Set targets that are both appropriate and achievable.
- Be sure to reward hard work and good performance.
- Remember that sometimes a simple thank you goes a long way.

ENGAGING WITH PEOPLE

- Show others that you respect and value their time.
- Give everyone a chance to contribute ideas, ask questions, and give feedback.
- Make sure everyone understands how their work contributes to the success of the company.
- Offer support and show a genuine interest in their overall wellbeing.
- Choose an office language and encourage everyone to speak it.
- Show positivity and professionalism in your interactions with others.
- Make sure everyone knows that they are a valued member of the team.
- Ensure everyone treats each other with respect, professionalism, and kindness.
- Remember, you're human. It's okay to tell stories and crack jokes.

STREAMLINING PROCESSES

- Be a positive presence in the office and try to always lead by example.
- Encourage punctuality and good time management.
- Let people improve at their own pace.
- Give people the chance to learn by delegating tasks.
- Strive for better results and encourage others to do the same.

PREVENTING FUTURE PROBLEMS

- Encourage people to have a positive attitude and a good work ethic.
- Offer support to those who are experiencing problems outside of work.
- Give people the chance to work from home or take time off if needed.
- Offer praise in public, offer constructive criticism in private.
- Look out for signs of bullying and address any issues immediately.
- Support people who fail at a task and teach them how to improve.
- Be gracious when accepting resignations and thank your colleagues for their hard work.

If you have any questions or suggestions, feel free to contact me at book@kentriboe.com

Acknowledgement

I would like to thank Sarah,
Who showed the greatest of patience to see this book come to life.

You've got my deepest appreciation for your help.